EMOTIONAL INTELLIGENCE
STYLE PROFILE

Dr. Jon Warner

HRD Press, Inc. ❖ Amherst ❖ Massachusetts

EMOTIONAL INTELLIGENCE STYLE PROFILE

This Emotional Intelligence Style Profile is designed to help you understand the way you apply your emotional intelligence style, preferences, and behavior. It can help you determine how appropriately and effectively you apply your knowledge and feelings in a given situation, and it is this understanding that forms the basis on which you can make adjustments in order to be more effective in the future, personally as well as professionally.

This instrument *will not* help determine your degree of emotional intelligence or your relative state of emotional health.

Each person uses his or her emotions and intelligence in different ways. One style is not better or worse than another. Therefore, there are no "right" or "wrong" responses. As you will see in this explanatory material, most everyone's responses to the questions at some point will fall within each of four broad emotional intelligence style quadrants. What that means is that in our day-to-day actions or behavior, we will draw to some extent on each of the four styles.

This is a self-scoring profile. Once you have responded to all the statements, you will be given instructions on how to plot your scores on the emotional intelligence grid shown on page 12. This will give you a graphic representation of your emotional intelligence style. Some general interpretive information has been included in the back of this booklet to help you determine whether you can increase your personal effectiveness by learning how to switch styles according to the demands of the situation.

Directions

On the next page, you will find 32 statements about behavior. For each statement, think about how you currently react in real situations. (Do not guess how you should act in the future.) Be sure to circle the letter that *most closely* applies to you, using the following scale:

T   **True for you**
PT **Partly true for you**
N   **Neither true nor false for you** (try to avoid this box when you can)
PF **Partly false for you**
F   **False for you**

Please use a ballpoint pen or a pencil to mark your answers on the Emotional Intelligence Style Profile Response Form (NCR form), so that all of your responses will come through clearly.

Emotional Intelligence Style: Questions

1.	I put other people's needs ahead of my own.
2.	I generally draw on past experience to help solve problems or make decisions.
3.	I try to avoid making snap judgments or quick decisions.
4.	I frequently try new ideas and options.
5.	I feel strongly about people's individual rights.
6.	I like to be seen as always reliable and dependable.
7.	I enjoy organizing people and resources whenever necessary.
8.	I often do things on impulse.
9.	I see myself as an effective peacemaker during times of conflict.
10.	I believe that some traditional values are extremely important.
11.	I like to suggest various courses of action to help solve problems or to overcome an obstacle.
12.	I studiously avoid work that involves a lot of detail.
13.	I enjoy social gatherings or events.
14.	I prefer having lots of time to plan ahead.
15.	I like to weigh alternatives carefully when I face complex situations or challenges.
16.	I enjoy taking big risks in my day-to-day decision making.
17.	I see it as my duty to help people who are less fortunate than I.
18.	I believe that consistency is more important than innovation.
19.	I like to slowly and carefully turn things over in my mind.
20.	I am more inclined to focus on tomorrow than today.
21.	I enjoy talking and getting to know new and different people.
22.	I have a strong sense of what is right and what is wrong.
23.	I like to prepare a list of my priorities carefully.
24.	I actively try to learn about new and creative ideas and concepts.
25.	I tend to worry about other people's problems or difficulties.
26.	I prefer to see everyone getting the chance to contribute democratically in group meetings or get-togethers.
27.	I often find myself drifting off or daydreaming.
28.	I see myself as a very good lateral thinker.
29.	I have a deeper or more "spiritual" relationship with some people.
30.	I like to establish sound systems and processes that can be easily followed.
31.	I operate on the principle *A place for everything, and everything in its place.*
32.	I prefer to put information into its wider context immediately.

Introduction

"Emotional intelligence" refers to the personal-management and social skills that allow us to succeed in our interactions with other people. Intuition, character, integrity, motivation, and communication and relationship skills are all part of emotional intelligence.

Emotional intelligence (also known as EQ) draws on two simple concepts: applying *knowledge* appropriately, and applying *feelings* appropriately. Being intellectually and emotionally astute or tuned-in to a particular situation or interaction *and* adjusting our behavior according to what we know and perceive—applying emotional intelligence—is considered an important factor in personal and professional success.

This instrument is concerned with how we generally apply our emotional intelligence. The model used is based on the belief that emotional intelligence is driven by motivation and the relative structure or flexibility of an individual's thinking about him- or herself and others. The model suggests that "applying knowledge appropriately" is fundamentally about analysis and intuition, and that "applying feelings appropriately" is about experience and expression.

A four-quadrant grid is used to help categorize responses and measure for style—the way a specific individual tends to apply his or her emotional intelligence. This model is shown on the next page.

The Grid

The first axis on the grid represents an individual's basic motivation or drive in terms of overall situational behavior. The Outcome end of the scale represents an individual focus predominantly on "tasks" or "results," and adoption of either an "analytical" or an "intuitive" approach to situations. The Belief end of the scale represents an individual focus predominantly on past experience and personal values, and adoption of either a "practical" or an "expressive" approach in terms of emotional intelligence.

The second axis on the grid relates to how structured the individual is in his or her approach to a situation and his or her behavior. The Controlled end of the scale represents an individual who generally focuses on facts and who is generally "systems-oriented." The Experimental end of the scale represents an individual who tends to be "open or flexible" and "feelings-centered" in his or her relationships with others.

When the two axes intersect, all four styles of emotional intelligence are shown on the grid: **Reflective, Conceptual, Organized,** or **Empathetic.** Most of us will tend to favor one or two styles in most circumstances.

Style and Emotional Intelligence

Each style has its advantages, and we are able to draw on them all at some time in our lives. There are situations, however, in which one specific style might be more effective than any of the others. In fact, the ability to apply all four styles appropriately is a factor in emotional intelligence; the more easily we can shift from our preferred style to one that might be the most appropriate for a specific situation, the more emotionally intelligent we are likely to become. Yes, *emotional intelligence can grow!*

This "balanced" use of our emotional intelligence takes practice. It starts with a strong sense of self-awareness, as well as motivation and an understanding of the quadrants we lean toward or away from (those are the ones we will need to focus on building). Once your individual results are plotted, use the Interpretation Notes to map out your improvement efforts.

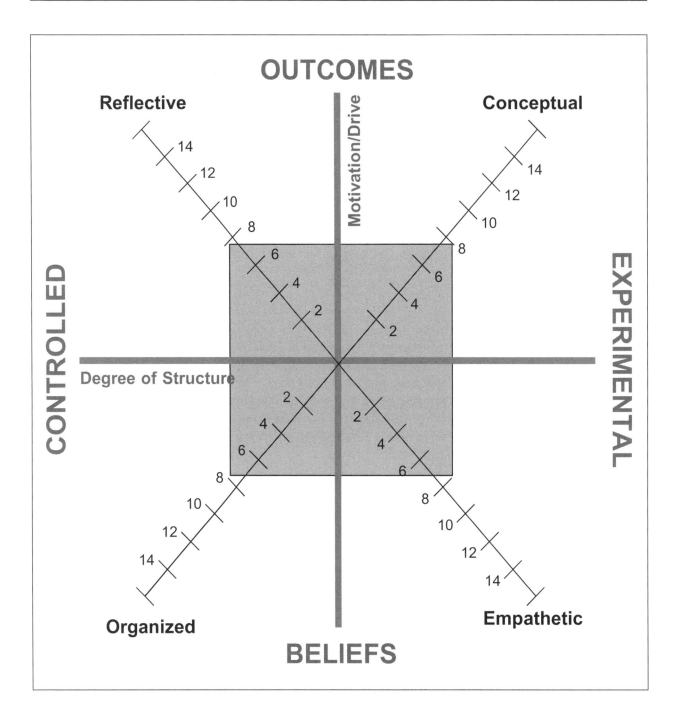

If an individual has developed the ability to draw on any of the four emotional intelligence styles at will, depending on which one is most appropriate for a particular circumstance, we say that he or she takes a "balanced" approach. The shaded area of the graphic on this page illustrates this ability to use all four styles equally; one or two might be all that is needed most of the time, but the individual represented here has learned how to "read" a situation or a mood and select the best of all four EQ styles before acting or reacting.

Scoring Your Instrument

If you separate the scoring sheet from the response sheet, you will see that your True, Partly True, Neither True nor False, Partly False, and False responses have translated into positive as well as negative numbers. Your first task is to total these numbers and enter them in the appropriate column sum boxes at the bottom of the page. (Add positive and negative numbers carefully.) You will end up with an overall score that is positive or negative, or even zero (with all the positives and negatives canceling out).

The four column sum boxes (Reflective, Conceptual, Empathic, and Organized) correspond to each quadrant in the emotional intelligence style grid. By translating these total column scores, you can now plot these numbers on the grid by making a mark on the relevant diagonal axis, counting out from the center. Each scale goes from 0 at the center to 16 at the end of the scale on the positive side (incremental points appear at 2, 4, 6, 8, 10, 12, and 14). The scale is also 0 to 16 on the negative side of the diagonal. If your score on the **Conceptual** is negative, for example, your mark should be made on the diagonal line in the **Organized** quadrant.

Most people will have a positive net score in all four quadrants, but some people will have a positive net score in only three or possibly two quadrants. This simply means that these individuals are highly unlikely to ever use the quadrants in which they do not score at all when dealing with most situations. This does not mean that they have no emotional intelligence in these quadrants. The emotional intelligence style that they generally use is likely to be driven from a narrow range of skills or competencies associated with this quadrant; for example, an individual scoring in only the **Organized** and **Empathetic** quadrants would be likely to have an internal or inward-looking focus on values and people-relationships, something that is not so important to people who are entirely **Reflective** and/or **Conceptual.**

Once you have all the points from your four column scores plotted on the grid, connect all the marked points with a straight line. Lightly shade in the resultant shape. Which quadrant is the most shaded? This is your primary indicated emotional intelligence style. Which is the largest area (your secondary indicated emotional intelligence style)?

The grid on the next page illustrates how response scores look when they are plotted.

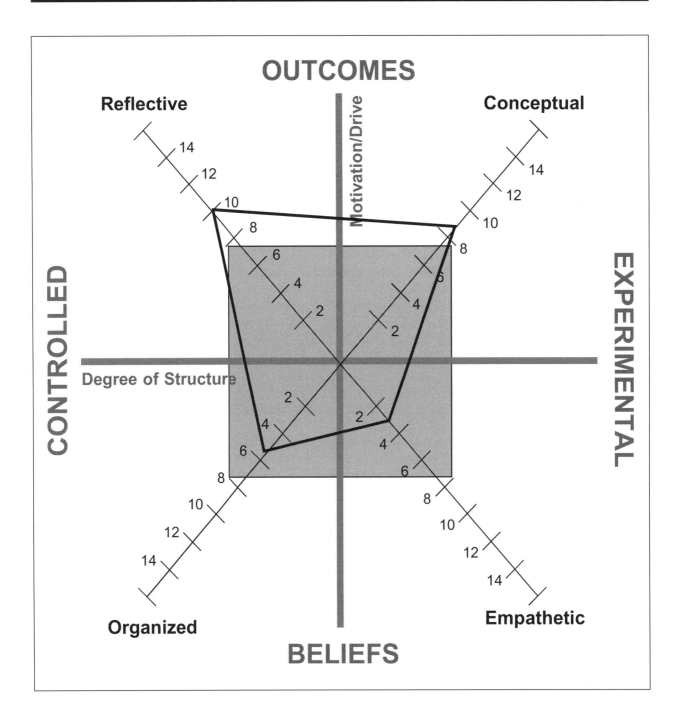

This individual's strongest emotional intelligence style quadrant is **Reflective** (their primary style), followed by **Conceptual** (their secondary style). Both of these scores are higher than the average quadrant scores in these segments. Their **Organizing** quadrant is their tertiary style. The **Empathetic** quadrant is the lowest-scoring area and therefore the one that ought to be evaluated and possibly improved.

Interpreting Your Results

The effective emotional intelligence grid has four quadrants, which each carry a general descriptive label. These are:

1. **Reflective**
2. **Conceptual**
3. **Empathetic**
4. **Organized**

These quadrants refer to the outcome descriptions of the four styles and the extent to which motivation comes from a desire for outcome or is based on belief. This is represented on two intersecting axes in a simple grid, drawn as follows:

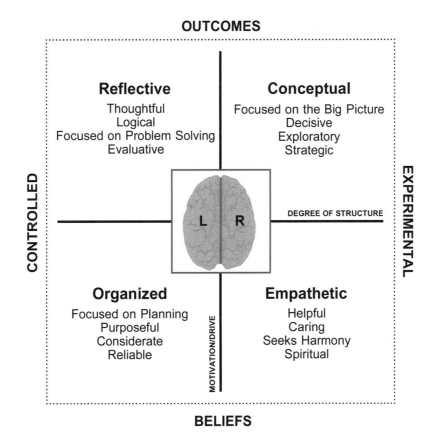

If the individual responds honestly to each of the questions, it is likely that one style preference will emerge. This clear tendency to use one style most of the time is generally referred to as the *primary* style. A *secondary* style will also emerge that is stronger than the remaining two styles. It is this pair of styles that the individual will adopt most often, shifting back and forth between the two easily, depending on how he or she perceives the situation. (It should be noted that the Reflective style and the Organized style are believed to be left brain-driven; Conceptual and Empathetic styles are generally considered to be right brain-driven).

Some situations will call for the use of all four styles: Reflective, Conceptual, Empathetic, and Organized. If the goal is to, say, achieve consensus among several individuals or to develop and discuss possible solutions to a multifaceted problem, having the ability to select from all four styles will be a clear advantage.

REFLECTIVE

In this high-structure, high-outcomes, or results-driven style quadrant, the individual is likely to focus on tasks but achieves his or her goals in a quiet, considered, ordered, and incremental or sequential manner. To do this, he or she will approach new situations by first collecting information that he or she can then logically analyze and evaluate carefully before he or she decides or acts.

The **Reflective** style type is predominantly interested in how the external world is structured and ordered and is therefore most concerned about gathering data and mentally sifting and reviewing it. The Reflective type consequently sees emotions, feelings, beliefs, and values only as observable behaviors or actions that should be noted and appropriately categorized, along with all other perceptions of external events or situations. In other words, levels of personal empathy and emotion are low or even nonexistent.

CONCEPTUAL

In this highly experimental, high-outcome, or results-driven style quadrant, the individual is likely to be task-focused, achieving his or her goals in a challenging, stretching, decisive, and nonlinear manner. To do this, he or she will approach new situations by sharing a variety of observations, ideas, and suggestions in order to stimulate people to think about new or different horizons. Some of these views will be sketchy and deliberately impulsive, but strongly defended.

The **Conceptual** style type is predominantly interested in how the external world can be understood in a range of different ways, and then changed or altered through action. New information helps to modify this person's view of the world. The Conceptual type sees emotions, feelings, beliefs, and values only as observable behaviors to be incorporated into his or her big picture of people and life in general.

ORGANIZED

In this high-structure, highly belief-driven style quadrant, the individual is likely to strongly value a world in which people can interact simply, fairly, and with certainty, and also purposefully seek to establish sound processes that others will find helpful to follow. To do this, he or she will approach new situations by communicating the importance of having clear processes and systems, personal competence, good planning, and discipline as a basis for an organized world in which people can operate in a calm, familiar, and well-ordered climate.

The **Organized** style type is predominantly interested in how the world of inner beliefs and the values of every individual can be accommodated in an orderly way, using a well-understood and practical set of parameters in which people can operate with confidence and certainty.

EMPATHETIC

In this highly experimental, highly belief-driven style quadrant, the individual is likely to have a strong need to understand and communicate with people at a social level, and to spend much of his or her time looking to extend and deepen his or her relationships with others. To do this, he or she will adopt a warm and gregarious approach to new situations and events in general, and strive hard to understand other people's inner feelings and views. The Empathetic type consequently likes to connect with others at an emotional level, and most enjoys relationships in which feelings are open and known (and outcomes and task goals are secondary).

The **Empathetic** style type is predominantly interested in how the world of inner feelings, beliefs, and values can be better understood. He or she is therefore likely to adopt an open, giving, and altruistic approach in the hope that it engenders the same response in others.

OUTCOMES

HIGH

Reflective

ADVANTAGES

- Likely to think deeply about issues.
- Likely to adopt a logical and analytical approach.
- Likely to approach problems systematically.
- Likely to evaluate complex alternatives.

DISADVANTAGES

- Might discount the feelings of others.
- Might see some strong beliefs as being poorly grounded in facts and evidence.
- Might come across as cool and aloof.
- Might dismiss all opinions and assumptions until there is hard "proof."

Conceptual

ADVANTAGES

- Likely to enjoy taking on large and complex issues and challenges.
- Likely to raise new and interesting options and possibilities to explore.
- Likely to be quick in selecting from a range of alternative options.
- Likely to cover a lot of ground in a short space of time.

DISADVANTAGES

- Might make decisions without much quiet or detailed consideration.
- Might not engage in any step-by-step planning or preparation.
- Might quickly "jump" from one issue to the next (in "skittish" fashion).
- Might not follow through; might fail to tie up loose ends.

CONTROLLED   EXPERIMENTAL

Motivation/Drive

Degree of Structure

Organized

ADVANTAGES

- Likely to value the development of clear systems and processes.
- Likely to look for widespread input from others in shaping a sound conclusion.
- Likely to see themselves as resolute and dependable.
- Likely to highly value practical experience.

DISADVANTAGES

- Might resist being pressured to decide or act.
- Might focus on the present much more than the future.
- Might not push the boundaries or stretch beyond known limits.
- Might impose controls where they are not wanted.

Empathetic

ADVANTAGES

- Likely to be generous of spirit and giving as a person.
- Likely to take time and trouble to understand people's feelings.
- Likely to avoid conflict and work hard to make peace.
- Likely to seek deeper and more meaningful relationships.

DISADVANTAGES

- Might take large amounts of time to understand other people's feelings; might ignore time constraints.
- Might use gut feelings, instinct, and hunches to form their views.
- Might trust easily and take people at face value.
- Might try to avoid difficult or unpopular decisions.

BELIEFS

Your Individual Score Page

If you have responded honestly and accurately to each question and plotted your individual "score," you are now ready to successfully apply what you have learned.

1. Review the characteristics of your primary and secondary styles. Try to think of one or two situations in which you probably used these styles.

2. Compare your mix of styles with the chart showing the "balanced" approach. Identify the style that you least tend to favor, and review its characteristics. Now recall a situation you did not handle so effectively and ask yourself whether or not one of these two "weaker" styles would have been of more help to you.

3. Determine whether or not your primary and secondary styles are right for the situations you generally find yourself in. If they are not, give some thought to adjusting your style or developing those that would be of more use to you.

As we said in the beginning, there are no "right" or "wrong" responses when you apply a particular emotional intelligence style. You use the information you have at the time in order to respond to the situation. Your responses will vary according to the situation. That said, you probably also want to be effective—to use the style that is comfortable for you and that will work to your advantage and help you achieve your objective.

Applying What You Have Learned from the Instrument

The good news is that this ability to be effective is within your reach! The essential value of any instrument is how well it indicates your personal way of operating or behaving. It should help you determine if there are areas that should be adjusted or changed, and then help you identify them.

You can get even more out of this instrument on emotional intelligence style if you have two or three friends or colleagues answer the questions based on how *they* see you. Average their scores and plot them on the grid as well; it will provide a snapshot of the style others believe you are practicing—how you come across to colleagues—and provide a good basis for strengthening your overall approach.

You can strengthen your emotional intelligence by becoming adept at using each of the four styles. Colleagues who appear to be strong in the use of styles you want to learn to apply can no doubt provide you with some tips to augment the suggestions on the next page.

Suggestions for Developing Your Emotional Intelligence

Fortunately, we can increase our EQ. Take advantage of these general suggestions to make greater positive use of each of the four styles of emotional intelligence. The more you successfully use all four quadrants to respond to situations, the more you increase your EQ and the more successful you will be, professionally and personally.

REFLECTIVE	CONCEPTUAL
Positive ways to use the *Reflective* Style:	**Positive ways to use the *Conceptual* Style:**
• Slow things down and encourage people to take their time before deciding or acting (including yourself). • Think about issues in a systematic, sequential, step-by-step fashion in order to better understand how things fit together. • Slowly and logically collect all the data that is needed in order to weigh the alternatives properly and make an informed decision. • Take the time to write down new or different approaches or solutions to present problems or challenges.	• Put specific and detailed issues into their broader context in order to better understand them. • Generate lots of new and interesting options and possibilities to help successfully deal with familiar issues and problems. • Deal with lots of issues or topic areas quickly and basically in the beginning. • Informally explore the possible future consequences of different scenarios or potential courses of action.

ORGANIZED	EMPATHETIC
Positive ways to use the *Organized* Style:	**Positive ways to use the *Empathetic* Style:**
• Approach situations in a quiet, considered, and controlled manner. Factor in the ideas and feelings of others. • Draw on what has been said and done in the past so that future actions are sensible and consistent. • Encourage individuals to develop systematic approaches and solutions that can be easily tracked and measured, in order to gauge overall success. • Focus on what you know for sure or what you believe to be true, rather than guess or make unfounded assumptions.	• Put other people's needs ahead of your own on a frequent basis. • Go out of your way to identify opportunities to bring people together in order to communicate and resolve any conflict or unhelpful differences. • Put yourself in other people's shoes so you will better understand how they are thinking or feeling. • Try to understand people at a deeper and even more "spiritual" level to appreciate their fundamental drives and motives.

Name: Date:

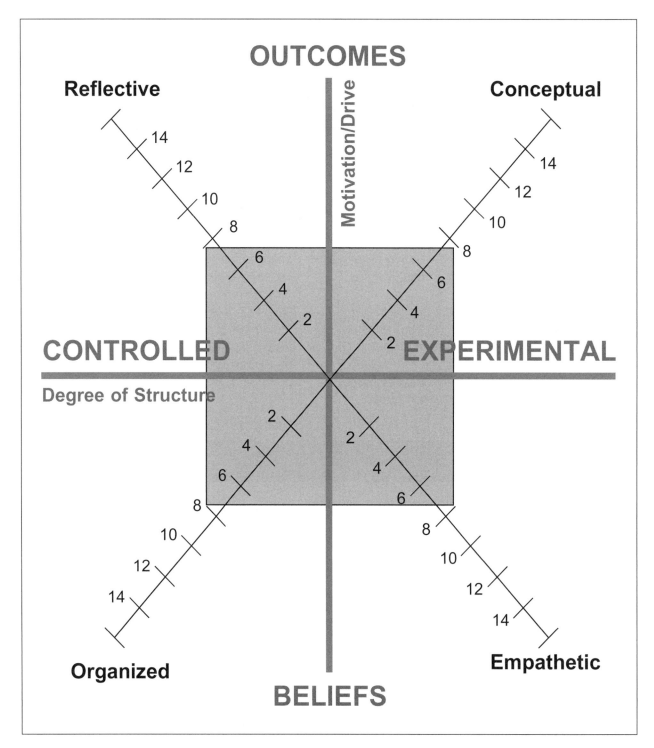

About the Author

Jon Warner has had over 20 years' experience in a number of major multinational companies in the United Kingdom, Europe, the United States, and Australia. This experience has included time as a senior staff member in human resources and a number of line roles with responsibility for large groups of people. During the last 5 years Jon has been involved in wide-ranging organizational consultancy and the pursuit of best practice leadership. This consulting has taken him into a number of major organizations such as Mobil Oil, the National Bank, BTR, Quantas, Gas and Fuel, United Energy, Air Products and Chemicals, Honda, Caltex, Dow Corning, Barclays Bank, and Coca Cola.

Jon Warner is also Managing Director of Team Publications Pty., Limited, an international training and publishing company committed to bringing practical and fun-to-use learning material to the worldwide training market. He holds a B.A. (honors) degree, a master's degree in business administration, and a Ph.D. in organizational change and learning. He now lives and works in the Gold Coast in Australia.